MW01623021

## RETAILER'S REVENGE

Wouldn't it be nice if just one day a year
We could have a sale day all nasty customers would fear
A chance to get back, a chance to get even
A reversal of roles, an opportunity to believe in!

To refuse to put up with the grief they give us
To argue right back, yell, scream, even cuss
To take no returns, give no refunds, no credits
To kick them out of our store isn't the worst they would get!

No more babysitting of children as <u>they</u> shop down the mall
No more using our phones, for that -hah- "emergency" call
Make them clean up their own mess - from the spills to the clothes
To laugh at their problems...anything goes!

A retailer's dream, avoiding their grief
A taste of their own medicine - what a great relief!

# CONTENTS

*Dedicated to:*

*Kevin*

*My brother, my touchstone, my believer,
he never doubted my capabilities, never
failed to encourage me, never
could be loved more...*

*Thank you*

# COMMON SENSE TO RETAILING

by

C. L. Nute, CMD

*Published by*
**The Retail Press**
**Columbia, SC**

Published by:
The Retail Press, P. O. Box 12554, Columbia, SC 29211

ISBN O-9645328-0-8
Library of Congress Catalog Card Number 95-67492

Anyone who has been in retailing for any length of time will probably chuckle upon reading Retailer's Revenge. We've all generally had our dose of unpleasant or nasty customers. By offering the best of everything, or more importantly by paying attention to detail, most problems often encountered by our customers and ourselves can be allieviated.

This retail guideline emphasizes just that - attention to detail. It is the little things that make a difference. As a marketing director, you may find these suggestions helpful when dealing with a store in trouble. You may even decide to have your own tenant education seminar using each chapter as a daily topic.

As a store retailer, whether you have been in the business 20 years or are just beginning your own, this guideline offers a "getting back to basics" course in retailing. A refresher course if you will. Many things that may be common sense to most, might have been forgotten. Many will be new ideas.

Ever mindful of our reason for being - our customer - this guideline will attempt to take you full circle. From basic operations and salespeople training, to advertising and customer service, managing all aspects of our time will become the key to unlocking a threshold of new opportunities, new awareness, and dollars in our cash registers.

# 1

# TIME MANAGEMENT

## HOW TO MANAGE YOUR TIME

Eat your P's everyday! That is, Proper Planning Prevents Poor Performance! Finding time to do your job, means you must make the time. Managing your time in a productive and efficient manner means that the job gets done on time, and gets done right the first time. There are many ways to manage your time - daily, weekly, and monthly.

In order to learn how to manage your time effectively, you need to take an inventory of how you manage your time now. You'll find there are certain characteristics when it comes to managing our time that many of us have in common. Such as: doing things we like before doing things we don't like; doing things that are scheduled rather than things that are unscheduled; we wait for deadlines to approach before we really hustle; we do small jobs before large ones; we do things that are easier first. The best way to find out how you manage your time is to write down what you do every day in fifteen minute intervals, as you do it. Do not wait and write it down at lunch or the end of the day. You need to write a synopsis of how you spend your time. In doing so, you'll find where you wasted your time. Ask yourself, "What was the goal of each thing I did? Did I achieve my goal? Why or why not? What areas of improvement need to be made?" When looking for these clues, ask yourself these questions:

- Are you delegating enough tasks?
- Are you delegating clearly what needs to be done and why?
- Are you attempting to do too much in a given time period?
- What went right/wrong?
- Are you disorganized?
- Are you understaffed?
- Are you too easily distracted by phones or visitors?
- Are you listening to your own instructions? I.e. are they clear?
- What time of the day was the least/most productive?
- What can you do to make better use of your time?
- Are you writing down a list of "to do's" or are you trying to mentally remember them?

R. Alex Mackensie's, Managing Time at the Top gives some excellent examples of time robbers, their causes and some solutions.

Once you have an idea of where you are wasting time it will be necessary to begin to counteract it. Begin by making sure you write down your goals - after all, if you don't write them down, how do you know what your goals are? How will you be able to measure where you are in relation to your goals? Next, learn to delegate more and procrastinate less. Avoid this by once again having specific goals. In terms of planning time, you may ask: "When should I delegate? When should I do it myself? Should I do a task now or can it wait until later?" Any decision making which occurs during the day will fall into one of these categories. (This of course assumes you do have someone to delegate to, and you aren't the sole worker involved.) Here is a simple formula to follow:

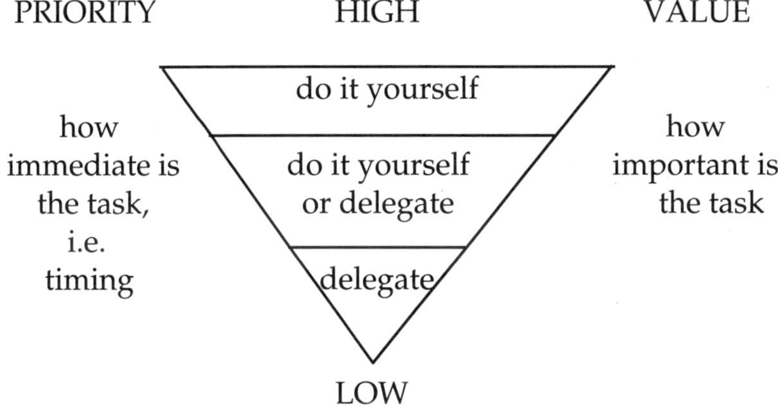


For example: A high priority/high value task should be completed by yourself; a high priority/low value task should either be completed by you or delegated; a low priority/high value task should either be completed by you or delegated; a low priority/low value task should be delegated.

Where do you go from here? Begin at the beginning. First determine what you plan to accomplish for the day, week, month. (Remember, a goal must be measurable and have a time factor. Example of a goal - read two books a month.)

Second, once you have a set goal (written down!) you need to determine what objectives are necessary to help you reach your goal. Also, what is the timing or proper sequence of those objectives. Break down objectives into a logical sequence of events. If you're doing a floor move for example, you must first decide what the new floor plan will look like and diagram it out on paper. Which of the objectives can then be delegated to your assistant; to your salespeople? For example:

GOAL - To achieve a sales volume of $5000 by the end of the week.

OBJECTIVES - Break down sales on a daily basis.
- Break down sales on an hourly basis.
- Give each employee an hourly goal.

You might even decide to create a sales contest as an incentive to help you reach your goal. Perhaps you might plan a floor move to feature your newest merchandise as an objective to help stimulate sales. Another objective would be to make sure to suggest additional merchandise on every sale made.

Third, assign authority and responsibility. Keep in mind when delegating who likes to do what. Maybe you have a salesperson who really enjoys doing displays. Selecting the right person for the job can be crucial to accomplishing your goal. Schedule them at the appropriate time and delegate the task to them.

Fourth, show others how <u>they</u> can do it. When delegating, make sure your people know the reason behind what they're doing, and when it's expected to be done. "Sally, we have a sales goal this week of $5000. In order to help us reach that goal you need to sell $60 per hour." It's a lot easier to keep good salespeople by keeping their job interesting. They need to know what's going on so they can be excited about their job, and will feel like a part of the team. It's up to <u>you</u> to keep them motivated. Proper delegation and reinforcement will do just that. Gaining their commitment to complete a task is essential to delegation working for all those involved.

## HOW TO MANAGE YOUR PEOPLE'S TIME

Again, when planning your time you must plan your people's time in order to ensure both everyday business as well as unexpected plans are being handled in the best manner possible.

Remember, you must begin with a prioritized "to do" list. Assign various responsibilities to employees to insure their completion by day's end. Daily and weekly schedules will help insure that tasks are handled on a timely basis.

Employee work schedules, if made on a regular basis, will avoid unnecessary changes. Time off should be asked for well in advance, and should be designated on a first come first serve basis.

If an employee requests time off after the schedule is made, he or she should be made responsible to find a substitute - per your approval of course. Unless an emergency arises, this should be adhered to. It will help avoid last minute changes as well as an uncovered floor.

If an employee tries to take advantage of changing the schedule on a consistent basis due to a 'hot date' or whatever else, an immediate stop to the privilege of schedule changing should be enacted. This will help avoid unfairness and help them to plan their own time in a more efficient manner. Plus, it will avoid headaches for you. Proper scheduling of both your time and the employees will make for a smoothly run operation.

## GETTING YOUR PEOPLE TO MANAGE THEIR OWN TIME

Proper Planning to Prevent Poor Performance can be taken from the work place into the home. It's easy enough to teach your people how to set goals - after all, you'll be an expert if you've followed the above steps! Plus, it may prove beneficial in helping the employee understand where you're coming from. Simply have them follow the same outline as shown above. When they understand the importance of setting and accomplishing their own goals, it will help in turn to keep the wheels rolling at work. Overall morale will soar. It is a great feeling knowing you've accomplished something you've set your mind to.

You may want to consider having a special meeting to teach your employees about goal setting:

- That planning ahead and communicating those plans with others will give them a viewing point - not a point of view.

- That they should work together to implement plans, and work separately to complete the whole.
- That follow through is essential to any task to learn how you can make it better the next time, i.e. things done right or wrong.

Teach your people how spending an extra 15 minutes a day to plan adds up to one extra month a year. Tell them not to base performance on what everyone else is doing, rather get everyone else to watch them. Repetition is necessary to be the best - look at athletes, they do the same thing everyday. The key is to make the 1000th time as exciting as the first.

Most importantly teach them to place a high value on the things they want to accomplish, and to work hard no matter how they feel. In so doing, they will know that what the mind can conceive, can be accomplished.

# 2

# SALESPEOPLE & STORE OPERATIONS

"REWARDS - Remember Excellence Will Always Require Devotion to Service." This phraseology has been adopted by many organizations throughout the country. Providing the proper service truly requires all aspects of a business, from the right merchandise and great customer service, to a clean store, filling in stock, and great employees.

## SALESPEOPLE - FINDING THEM

Finding salespeople is never an easy task. Finding the right salespeople is the real qualifier that makes it especially tough. So, where do you find them? Some people may suggest you take out an ad, not necessarily a bad idea, but then you have to wade through all the undesirables to get to the better ones.

You could of course put a sign in the window and hope someone off the street will come in and apply. But then, have you seen what's out on the street lately?

Enough said. The best sources of personnel hiring are through your friends, business acquaintances and associates.

They generally know good people - after all, they know you don't they? Also, don't forget to look in your own back yard. Customers that shop with you regularly, obviously are already excited about the merchandise as well as your store. They may make excellent employees!

## RECRUITING

Have you ever been in another retail store and were particularly impressed by the salesperson who waited on you? Ever wonder why that person couldn't be working for you? Well it's probably because you haven't asked them!

As managers/owners you should make weekly tours of your other neighboring stores. This is whether you're located in a mall or downtown. Some of the best salespeople I've ever found were working for other retailers. Think about it, there's some credibility there since they already have a sales job.

I have gone in and talked with other managers, assistants, and salespeople. When talking about business, their merchandise, etc., you can feel them out about how happy they are in their present job. You can determine their future goals, their overall attitude, plus get some inside scoop on how their sales are doing.

Many times you can lure these people to work for you through various means: better pay, benefits, working conditions, etc. Many will work for you just to get a discount on your goods. There are also situations where they can work for two people at the same time, as long as there is no conflict of interest.

If you are a shoe store, your business presents no conflict to a record store, clothing boutique, or food merchant. It may mean being a bit more flexible in scheduling, but it will be worth it if it means dollars in your register.

## INTERVIEWING

This brings up the next step of finding a great salesperson - the interview. There are many traits of a good employee. It's up to you during the interview to find out whether or not the applicant has these traits. How the applicant comes dressed will tell you a lot about who you're hiring. Do they bring children? Baby-sitting/child care may be a problem. Were they late? Did they call and let you know?

Put the applicant at ease when they arrive. Having them tell you about themselves, is one way. Sometimes a simple compliment helps. Some interviewers prefer to explain the interview process as an ice breaker. Whichever method you choose, you should plan a constructive approach. Let the application form guide the interview.

Listen! It's amazing what you may pick up on. Give, as well as get information. Making a wise decision can be tough, and not as obvious as it may seem. You might have genuinely liked the applicant, but perhaps he just wants a job and is not necessarily interested in retail. Will his appearance and attitude have a favorable impression on your customers? Does he/she have potential to grow? Are there any personal problems that may effect his/her performance? Do check references! It's amazing at times what you may learn. I was told by a fellow manager "off the record" that my candidate was suspected of theft but had quit before anything was proven. Certainly food for thought!

## SALESPEOPLE - TRAINING THEM

Once you have found your ideal person, it is now up to you to begin the molding process. You must conform them to your and your company's way of doing business. Give them a history lesson on where and how your company got started. Get them excited about who they work for. They need to understand that they are a vital part of a growing and dynamic team, regardless of their job description. They should take pride in their job whether they are the janitor or the president.

All the gears must work together if the machine (your company) is to run smoothly. Get them to care about their job from the start. This means training, and sometimes lots of it. They must be trained on store policies, the register, merchandise, stock and store maintenance, and of course - customer service.

Train by example! Remember the old childhood saying, "monkey see, monkey do"? People believe what they observe. Take the time to train new salespeople. If something comes up and you're too busy, postpone their hiring day or delegate the task to another. On many occasions I have paired off a new employee with the number one salesperson in sales, or in display, or in merchandising. These traits are not always found on the same person. Let the trainee know why they're being paired off. "Sharon, this is my number one salesperson, and he/she is going to help you today." You'll find on most occasions they're more comfortable working with a peer. Not only that, but the trainer feels great knowing that you think so highly of them and will be careful to "tell all" to the trainee on the subject at hand. As a manager, follow up periodically. Ask the trainee a few questions to be sure nothing has been left out, and that they understand what's been taught so far. You'll probably find by the end of the day not only has valuable knowledge been gained, but also a new friend has been made that the new employee feels comfortable asking questions of and working with.

It's crucial during training, and throughout their career for that matter, that your salespeople know what's expected of them. Overall they should understand that selling is their number one priority. The customer always comes first. However, they must also understand there are many non-selling stages of their job which must also take place, if the number one priority - the customer, is to be made happy.

## GENERAL MAINTENANCE

There are many different phases of the non-selling side

of retail. We'll begin with the most basic one, cleanliness and upkeep. General store maintenance, when completed on a regular basis will help reduce maintenance costs in the long run. Store cleaning lists such as what to do, and when to do it - whether before opening or after closing, should be posted and referred to on a daily basis. Don't become too easily satisfied with the cleanliness of your store, or the cleanliness will become mediocre if you do. Insure the store is clean - everyday. Fixtures should be polished/dusted on a daily basis. Floors vacuumed. Mirrors, glass, and chrome should be free of fingerprints. Tasks such as dusting merchandise, and emptying trash should also be handled daily. It will not only make your store safer, but will present the merchandise better. No customer wants to handle merchandise, or purchase it, for that matter, that has become soiled due to poor housekeeping. Again, these tasks can be performed before, during or after store hours. However, you should <u>never</u> vacuum during store hours. The noise is most obnoxious and will drive customers away. Should a spill occur during the day, use a carpet sweeper or a broom; something quiet that won't disturb your customers.

Every morning before your store opens you should walk to the front of your store and look for any mishaps. This means any missing or damaged signs, burned-out lights, incomplete displays, etc. These should be replaced, fixed or whatever else may be necessary <u>before</u> you open up. As you move through your store, see it as a customer would, making sure it looks fresh, appealing and in order.

Weekly maintenance items, such as cleaning the bathroom should be assigned to you and your employees on a rotating basis. This will avoid any unfairness.

Monthly maintenance for bigger tasks are generally best left to the professional. This includes items such as changing air conditioner filters, and the like.

Spring and Fall cleaning will also require an assignment of tasks. These jobs generally are bigger in demand of your time and energy. Tasks such as: the cleaning of your outside store sign; dusting ceiling tiles around air conditioner vents; cleaning your store gate or the store's carpet; are all bigger requirements that should be handled at this time.

General maintenance is a big undertaking for a store, but is best handled when broken down into an organized approach. Listing various tasks by daily, weekly, monthly, or semi-annual schedules will insure they are not forgotten.

## STOCKKEEPING

One of the most important characteristics of a store is its merchandise. It helps to identify itself and who its customers are. Or perhaps even who its customers would like to be. Whether the customer is male or female, large or small, traditional or trendy in taste, the type of merchandise presented will tell its own story, reflect its own identity. The way the merchandise is presented will also reflect an identity. Sometimes it helps to even change one. Ever see the "traditional" blue suit displayed with a 'flair for life' boldly colored scarf? Customers buy something based on a perception of themselves. The bit of a renegade would snatch at the chance to stand out in the office crowd. But, just as it's hard to tell a story without words, it's hard to sell an image without merchandise. Therefore, it's important to keep merchandise well stocked.

Stockkeeping, an important key to your store's well being, is composed of various different segments. Some stores hire people specifically for these various tasks. Other stores rely on their salespeople. Still others have a combination of both. Whichever the case, it's important to lay some ground rules.

First, stock should be checked on a daily basis. Remember, if goods are to be sold, they must first be seen. Customers cannot second guess what is in your back room. However, stockkeeping is always secondary to customer service. Keeping stock neat is never more important than a customer. If an item/size is sold out, it should be noted so refills, if available, can be obtained. Filling in stock as it is sold is vital to the proper flow of goods. Many times if a customer can't find an item, a sale is lost. Don't assume they will ask for what they can't find. They are so accustomed to going into stores where everything is "out on the floor", they don't always ask for help, or have time to wait while you check "in the back". Believe me, there are times when I've waited on a salesperson when I began to feel like their back room must have been three miles down, and four flights up!

Second, as stock is filled in, it's important to insure proper rotation. This means the older goods are sold first. This is especially important concerning food items, or seasonal merchandise such as swimwear. Rotation of goods also applies to getting newer merchandise out front. Make sure certain fixtures in the front of your store or department are filled in first. This helps to keep your merchandise looking new and fresh.

Third, when filling in, make sure you don't leave stock boxes either in the aisles, or unattended. The same goes for any trash you may have accumulated while filling in. Not only will these points make your store appear more aesthetically pleasing, but for safety purposes you will avoid potential hazards. Boxes, slippery plastic and pins can cause falls or other unnecessary injuries. It can be difficult enough keeping merchandise filled in at times without compounding the situation by being careless while you do it. As you're distributing the merchandise, make sure the fixtures are clean and hangers are hung in the same direction all the way around. The same type of hangers should be hung together. That is, don't mix plastic and wire shirt hangers. Ideally, nor should you mix shirt and pant hangers. Rather, keep them on separate arms of a four-way.

Fourth, displays should be kept clean and fresh, be attention-getting, and should always be filled in. They should tell a story. They should also be changed frequently. Never leave a display unfinished. If something has been removed to make a sale, be sure it gets filled in again. After all, two-thirds of all buying decisions are made while in a store. The better your picture, the better your sales. (More on displays will follow later.)

As with displays, merchandise on shelves and fixtures should be filled in. For many businesses, the bottom line is based on dollars per square foot. That is, the total dollars in sales divided by the square footage of the store. It's important therefore, that the square footage of the store not be filled with half-full or empty racks. (Exceptions to this rule are often made in designer lines of merchandise. Several items per tee-stand are said to give an air of exclusivity.) Think safety! Fixtures left empty can be a hazard. Someone can easily be injured or knock over an unbalanced rack.

Finally, when the merchandise is placed on the sales floor make sure it's presented properly. Buttons should be buttoned. Tissue and pins should be removed, otherwise you'll find them all over your floor. Goods should be properly hung, folded or stacked, whichever the case may be.

Some stores have full time salespeople whose main responsibility is seeing to this task. A word of caution here, even stock people should be courteous and helpful when on the sales floor. Take the time when hiring them to be sure that their sole purpose in life is not to sling merchandise out, ignoring the world around them. They too must be able to communicate and help a customer in need. Doesn't it make sense that since they handle the stock they should know something about it? They are, after all, a representative of your store.

Proper stockkeeping will ensure a smooth flow of goods from stockroom to sales floor to customer. In addition to stocking the merchandise, it's important to know about the merchandise. Some basics to learn are: fabric content; colors and sizes available; cost; how it washes and wears; will it shrink - how much; if out of an item can it be ordered from another store; etc. Its special features, what it goes with, and where it's located on the sales floor are also important. For example, what's the difference between Kodak and Fuji film, 14kt and 18kt gold, or a cubic zirconia and a diamond? Learning information about the merchandise can be obtained in store manuals, labels in garments, or by talking with managers, buyers, or fellow personnel. Another great medium is magazines. The better informed a salesperson is about something, the better they can answer a customer's questions and insure a sale. After all, if the salesperson doesn't know about it, what makes you think the customer will?

## SECURITY

Another segment of non-selling is loss prevention. This means not only keeping an eye out for shoplifters, but avoiding losses due to damaged fixtures, dirty fixtures, or just overall lack of care when handling garments. All these losses will reduce your bottom line - which is profits.

One of the most important reasons to keep your store orderly is to discourage shoplifters. They will assume you are as lazy about security as you are about the appearance of your store. If something is taken, how could you be sure what it was if merchandise is presented helter skelter? Another way to discourage shoplifters is excellent customer service. Greet everyone! Use eye contact. Shoplifters fear being recognized. If they think they will be recognized, that you will remember that they have green eyes not brown, brown hair not blond, as well as what they were wearing, etc., they won't be as inclined to try to steal from you. Wide aisles, good lighting, low displays, and a minimum of hidden areas will also help to increase a shoplifters fear of being caught. Preventing theft of goods or cash is an everyday undertaking.

As much as 65% of all thefts occur by your own employees!

You'd be amazed at some of the ways people will steal from you. Here are several things to keep an eye on in your store that will help prevent stealing both internally and externally.

1. Watch your garbage. Employees may try to conceal goods in it and then offer to take it out and give the goods to a friend, or put them in their car.
2. Make sure all outgoing packages and purses are inspected - including your own.
3. Keep your back door locked.
4. Check incoming and outgoing shipments. Don't allow truck drivers to handle them unescorted.
5. Don't place valuable or portable merchandise near entryways.
6. Keep keys separate from locks.
7. Lock your locks when not in use to prevent them from being switched. Thieves can replace your lock with theirs in order to gain access. After the theft, they replace your lock and you are none the wiser.
8. Rotate security guard's schedules to prevent them from a theft alliance with an employee.
9. A snapping sound of a hanger may mean someone is trying to conceal goods. Check it out!
10. Check the safe and all doors before you leave to ensure they are secure.
11. Don't allow employees to ring up their own merchandise.
12. Check your markups and markdowns carefully. This will avoid either ticket swapping or thieves taking their own markdowns.
13. Only allow authorized personnel to handle refunds.
14. Keep an eye on teenagers, especially in groups, they're responsible for as much as half of all shoplifting.
15. Make it clear that <u>anyone</u> caught shoplifting will be prosecuted fully under the law.
16. Keep an eye on what goes in and out of dressing rooms.
17. Keep track of hangers. If you found an empty hanger

in a dressing room, how would you know whether something was sold or stolen?

If you suspect someone of shoplifting, stay cool. The better you handle yourself and the situation, the better your chances of prosecution. Or, heaven forbid, if you've made a mistake, the better your chances of avoiding a lawsuit. Question your suspect using leading questions. "Is there anything else?" "Would you like to have that wrapped?" Many will pull an item out with an "oh, I almost forgot". For the shopper who eats a candy bar, "Did you want the candy bar rung up separately?"

If someone grabs and runs, depending on store policy, do not follow them. Call security or the police immediately and be prepared to give a full description of the thief and what you suspect was taken and its value. Most policemen will advise you not to follow in case the thief pulls out a weapon. Losing a $50.00 sweater is no measure for you losing your life.

If a suspect is apprehended before leaving the store, try to avoid handling them. Many have claimed assault charges. Never leave the suspect, nor should you be left alone with the suspect.

Whether or not the thief is arrested at that time, be sure to write a detailed account of what happened. Don't leave anything out! Sometimes, if it goes to trial, it may take as long as six months or more and you may forget some of the details if you don't write them down.

Remember, your most important key when it comes to theft, is prevention. Know your store policies in relation to procedures to prevent theft. Contact your local authority to ensure you know what your rights are if a theft should occur. But most importantly remember, the best source of prevention is excellent customer service!

The proper training of your salespeople in each of the non-selling areas will ensure that the 'behind the scenes' aspects are all running smoothly. If one was creating a play, those 'behind the scenes' non-selling areas, would in fact be your stage. Now that your stage is set, your salespeople - the actors- are now ready to rehearse (more training) their most important part. They need to learn their part well in order to get the audience - your customer, to respond accordingly - that means buy!

In training your employees to sell, they must learn five essential steps which are:

1. Greet the customer.
2. Determine the customer's needs.
3. Present the merchandise.
4. Overcome objections.
5. Close the sale/add on.

The minute your customer enters the store he/she should be greeted - no matter what, within three to five seconds. Regardless of whether you're doing stockwork, cleaning, or waiting on another customer - smile, nod your head, or acknowledge them with a friendly hello. It's very simple isn't it? You have now begun with **Step 1** of the selling process - the greeting.

When greeting your customer, avoid the question, "May I help you?" I guarantee that if you ask this question, 99% of the time your customer's response will be, "No thank you, I'm just looking". I often wonder what people would say if this phrase was stricken from the English vocabulary. Have you ever noticed how sometimes even though all you say is, "Hello, how are you doing today?" some customers rush right back with, "I'm just looking!" as if they're afraid you are going to try to force them to buy something? This could be an indication that this customer had an unpleasant experience with a pushy salesperson before. Your sales pitch must be credible to win a customer over. You have to get the customer to believe in your product and/or you in order to sell them. Now, this isn't hard to do, but it does require a slightly different approach.

Let's back up for a minute and give some good opening statements to begin "feeling out" our customer so we can determine their needs. The merchandise approach is one type of opening. This is where you build your rapport by zoning in on the qualities/characteristics of the merchandise they are looking at, such as:

- "Isn't that a beautiful sweater? Did you notice it's machine washable and dryable?"
- "Aren't the colors in that skirt pretty? We have some great blouses that match it too."
- "That blow dryer has three settings and comes with a styling brush."

Many stores use a special of the day or particular item they are trying to push.

- "Did you know all our kitchen utensils are 30% off today?"
- "Have you seen our new snake skin pumps? We just got them in today and they are really hot!"

Some salespeople feel more comfortable complimenting a customer on something about them personally.

- "I love your haircut! Who did it?"
- "That's a great looking blouse!"

After all, complimenting someone on a prior purchase - in a sincere way, makes them feel good about themselves, and they will feel immediately comfortable with you.

Then of course there's the more traditional greeting. Not as original, but it <u>can</u> work.

- "Was there anything special for yourself you were looking for?"

Regardless of the approach you use, make a habit of introducing yourself. "Hi, my name is Brenda, can I help you find your size?" Avoiding becoming another nameless, faceless, entity is one way to give credibility to your sales pitch. It also helps the customer remember who waited on them during a busy day. This is a great idea if you work on a commission!

There will be some customers that want to be left alone. They don't want your help unless it's to unlock a dressing room or get an item out of the stockroom. Your best bet is to leave them alone. Let them know if they do need assistance you'll be right there. Point out several key items in the store as you send them on their way to browse. A sale rack in the back, or new merchandise just received, are just some ideas. Encourage them to take their time, and look around. Try an occasional comment about the merchandise they're looking at. Don't hound them, but do let them know you're keeping an eye on them. This is a good idea especially for security purposes.

Practice the various greetings and use the one you feel most comfortable with.

In **Step 2** - determine your customer's needs, you must LISTEN! and listen completely! If you don't listen, the customer will become frustrated with you and won't buy anything. Many times a customer will tell you in detail, what they want.

- "I want a red party dress, easy to care for, between $100 and $200."

Sometimes, they will give generalities and the rest is left up to you.

- "I'm looking for a party dress."

Ask questions at this point. Once you have an idea, take the customer to the merchandise, don't direct traffic.

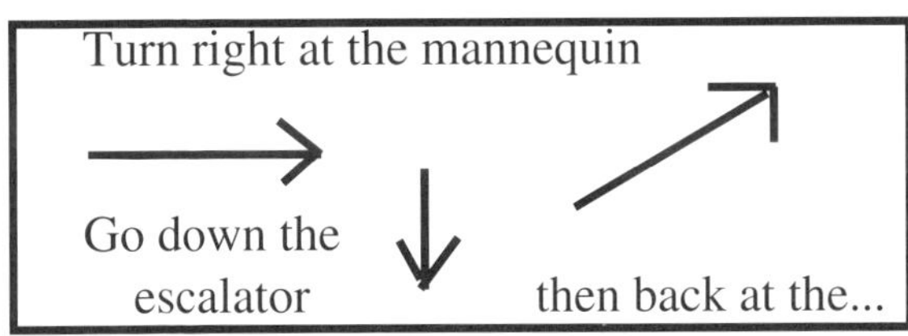


Obviously it's important to know your store's layout, so you will know where said merchandise is to be found. If you work in a department store and can't leave your area, do direct your customer to the proper area. Call ahead to tell the salesperson that your customer is coming and what he/she is looking for.

If you don't have what the customer needs, offer suggestions for substitutes. Make a list of items requested and the number of times it's requested. It may be possible to order it from the manufacturer, or get it from another store in your chain.

When presenting the merchandise to your customer - **Step 3**, let the customer examine it. Listen again here. What are their reactions to what you show them. Watch for non-verbal motions as well. Present its selling points. It's very important to show its varied uses. Generate excitement by getting the customer involved. Let them touch the merchandise. Again, know what sizes are available, its price, its care, what goes with it, etc., and relay this information to your customer.

Overcoming objections - **Step 4**, shouldn't invite a sparing match. Once again it's important to listen carefully to what your customer is saying. Answer the issues one at a time. Is it price, or is it quality? Is it the fit? Is it the color? Whatever it may be, you need to address it fully, and resolve it, before you can move on to achieving your sale.

If you have performed Steps 2 and 3 effectively, you will

find that your customer will not have any objections, and you can move right along to **Step 5**, closing the sale. There are several points to be covered when closing. First, in closing the sale you must first ask for the sale. "May I ring this up for you?" is one obvious and simple way. Second, you should spend time with your customer encouraging them that they have made the right decision. "Mrs. Brown, I just know you are going to be the hit of the party in this new dress." Making them feel comfortable about their purchase is a sure way of getting them to shop with you again. Third, you should suggest add-on or additional merchandise at this point.

Although many salespeople seem to resist this step, it is truly quite easy once you get the hang of it. It becomes a natural part of the sales process once practiced several times, and once the salesperson becomes comfortable with it. Asking "Will there be anything else?" isn't good enough. It's not very specific. "Would you like a pair of socks to go with those pants?", not only is specific, but also plants an idea in the customer's mind that they might not have considered before but "Now that you mention it..." Bang, the add-on sale is made.

The easiest way to suggest additional merchandise is to try and complement the original purchase being made. Here are some quick suggestions:

| When purchasing a | suggest this add-on |
|---|---|
| man's shirt | tie |
| sandwich | soft drink or chips |
| pair of earrings | matching necklace |
| sweater | pair of pants to match |
| suit | blouse |
| pair of shoes | purse to match |
| set of glasses | drink stirrers |
| gourmet cheese | bread, crackers, or wine |
| microwave | microwave cookbook |

This list is endless. But remember, you first must ask!

After flowing beautifully through the sales steps, please don't fumble the closing by asking, "Will that be cash, check or charge?" Ugh!! It is much more polite to ask "How do you wish to pay for this?" Or, if your store is trying to push its own credit card, you might ask "Would you like to charge this on your ABCD card?"

The final step to closing the sale is thanking the customer. Not only should you thank them by name, but you should encourage them to return. Many salespeople even request the customer ask for them by name when they return. Not only is this an asset when sales are commissionable, but also lets the customer know you enjoyed helping them.

Get to know your salespeople as fully as possible during training. This will help not only in keeping a good rapport with them, but when you learn what makes them tick you will know how to keep them motivated. When you keep them motivated - you keep them!

## SALESPEOPLE - KEEPING THEM

As was stated before, it's crucial that your salespeople know what's expected of them. This can be half the battle of keeping them motivated. Someone who is motivated is, or can be, a self starter. In Thomas Connellan's book, <u>Growing People Into Self Starters</u>, a self starter is: a consistently high performer; one who seeks growth and new responsibilities, and is an inspiration to others. Mr. Connellan also remarks on three steps to creating a self starting environment. First, create positive or high expectations. Expectations influence results. Second, set responsibilities and goals. What is the goal and what is the employee's responsibility in achieving that goal? Do they know it? Third, is feedback and applause. Give it and get it.

Remember that 'idle hands lead to idle chatter' which leads to idle everything, including sales! Keep your salespeople busy! There should never be a salesperson in your store who isn't busy. If they have nothing to do, send them home. Why pay someone to be a warm body? Delegate work and show others how they can do it. Be aggressive, and by example stimulate others to keep your pace. Make sure you periodically follow up training, especially if business is slow. It's a great opportunity to brush up an employee on a skill. Improving basic job skills can be a great motivational tool. Perhaps an area where an employee is weak can be strengthened by first, getting back to basics, then expounding on what they've learned by making improvements. Be sure to recognize that even you as a manager may not have all the right moves, or all the right answers. In recognizing each employee as an individual you'll learn to respect differences. Maybe an employee is a great salesperson but is weak in stockkeeping. Make improvements in this area their new goal.

Store maintenance can be fun if you approach it with the right attitude. Don't be a slave driver. It can be okay for your people to talk and work at the same time. It certainly can make the task at hand more enjoyable. Just make sure it doesn't get out of control - especially if a customer is around. Do not stand around while your employees are working. Make sure you too are performing. Nothing is more deflating to an employee than to have a manager hand out jobs, and then stand around smoking a cigarette because they feel the employees need supervision. First of all, if you have to watch your employees that closely, they shouldn't be working for you to begin with. It's pretty demoralizing when you make an employee clean the bathroom, while you dust the cash counter. Never let your employees think that you believe you're too good to do "that kind of work". You should be perceived as one of the team which means you should do some of the dirty work yourself.

Keeping your employees performing well generally means paying them well. Unfortunately, it isn't always feasible for some smaller stores. There are ways to get around this. Some stores rely on a partial commission. For example, once an employee has reached a minimum sales goal, everything following that which is sold, a commission is received. Whether it's 1% or more, it can be a nice incentive.

PM's or prize money is another incentive. This is a bonus paid for selling a particular item. An employee might receive 50 cents each time they sell a designer blouse.

Weekly or weekend sales contests are generally lots of fun. Select a particular item, say an accessory such as socks. The employee who sells the most receives a free pair. It's amazing how competitive people can be when there's something in it for them. In this case, it's recognition among their peers as being the best, as well as the prize itself. Obviously, you need to work out details so part-timers have a fair go at it against the full-timers.

Give employees recognition for a job well done. Most importantly, do it publicly! Whether it's a big poster at the time clock...

Congratulations Cathy!
#1
Salesperson
For the month of July
Way to Go!!!

...or an announcement during a meeting. If you have to criticize, make sure you do it privately and constructively. Reset goals as necessary, set a follow up date to review, and stick to it! Your employees will feel you don't really care if you don't.

In teaching your employees, you too will learn new things. Pass it along. There is a great feeling watching someone you hired as a part-timer go on to be promoted to store manager. The cycle continues as they teach what you taught, and so on. People who know there is future growth ahead of them will work a little harder. So whether the motivation lies in money, career, or another area of growth, you must do whatever you can to make a job interesting. Not only will your employee turnover reduce significantly, but you will also find many people knocking at your door for a chance at opportunity!

# 3

# YOUR CUSTOMERS & YOUR COMPETITION

## YOUR CUSTOMER - ATTRACTING THEM

Attracting customers to your store can be accomplished in a variety of ways. Advertising, effective storefront displays, good customer service, etc. Let's begin by addressing the customer passing by. Your prospective customer will get their first impression from the "look" of your storefront and interior.

It's a known fact that you have just three to five seconds to attract the attention of a passer-by. An attractive storefront draws customers like a magnet. This means your storefront must be attention getting. Therefore, a good deal of thought and effort should be given to making your store attractive, pleasant, and inviting.

How, you ask?

Simple. Your storefront must be clean, bright and cheerful, have proper signage, and interesting displays. Most importantly, it should avoid those vultures. You know, those vultures? They are employees, hanging out at the storefront, watching the world go by when they should be busy working. They appear to be waiting for that foolish unaware customer to come in so they can be pounced-upon and forced to buy something they neither need nor want. Customers will leave your store dazed and confused, not quite sure what happened to them yet cognizant enough to realize they will never go back!

Anyhow, getting back to your storefront, several points concerning display windows should be remembered. First, decide on your approach or theme.

- Are you going to introduce something new? Be it a new fashion, new color, new season or classification, you need to determine what will be the most effective.
- Are you going to reinforce an ad? Plan to show the merchandise and a copy of the ad, preferably blown up.
- Perhaps the time is right to tie in a local charity or civic campaign to let the community know you're a part of it.

Once the approach to the window has been determined, several techniques can be used to help pull it all together. Remember, no matter how good a product may be, if it isn't presented properly or dramatically in a way which inspires an individual to buy, it will not sell. Sometimes it helps to think of what the merchandise can do, rather than thinking of it as inanimate. Give character to those inanimate objects by placing them in a life-like situation.

For example, making people out of clothing, combining tops and bottoms in action moves, adding props such as a pair of skis with ski wear. Your window should tell a story. These grapes and wine graphics help to impact this store's visibility...

Once again, all items should be similar or should tie together somehow, such as coffee pots, coffee cups and coffee beans; or denim jeans, hiking boots, and flannel shirts. Backdrops or props are important to help pull your ideas together and should be consistent with the theme selected. However, avoid overpowering the merchandise that's presented by paying too much attention to non-merchandise factors. You should choose all items to be displayed carefully. Make sure when they are displayed they are secure. This is to avoid not only theft but to use safety precautions so a display won't fall over and cause damage or injury.

Giving your display window a little originality will help it be distinctive. Let's face it, motivating your customer towards a closer look at the merchandise and planting a yearning to buy is, after all, your main objective. Standing out from the competition is the best way to do this.

Some final points to remember; a clean, well lighted display window can make a dramatic difference. Fingerprints on glass are a sign people have been looking at your window. Be happy about them but don't leave them there! Avoid hand painted signs, they distract from the unified display. Plus, they generally look unprofessional. Try combining basic and novelty items for a more interesting effect. Make sure the window has a sense of balance or symmetry. That is, if the display were cut in half, equal parts would be on either side.

Part of catching your customer's attention in addition to an attractive window, is to have an overall appealing storefront. Gates should be rolled up completely, glass fronts should be clean, store signs should be on and working properly. If a letter on your sign isn't working, turn it off and call your electrician. Most customers don't like winking lights from a sign and most leases don't allow them anyway.

Many storefronts don't have a display window. In this situation most of the same guidelines can still apply as far as telling a story.

This does not necessarily mean you should place 300 red sweaters up in the front of your store. Rather, create mini sections filled with merchandise that will draw the customer into your store. Leaving blank walls or sparsely filled racks in your storefront, tells the customer you're out of merchandise.

Look at your store from a customer's perspective. Walk away from it, down the hall or across the street - how does it look now? What's the first thing you see? Does it attract you? Is the color scheme suitable?

The following is an incident that happened to me.

> There was a store located in a mall called Karl's Klothes. Mall management wanted to discuss with them the possibility of sprucing up their store. It was in desperate need of new carpet and a paint job, especially when compared to their competitors. There were several new ladies fashion stores in the mall, plus several of the older stores were getting remodeled - new paint, new carpet, and some structural changes on the inside.
>
> Karl's was located on a pop-out storefront, making it appear to be a corner store. You could see the store from halfway down the mall. I went to speak with the store manager, Edna, and her district manager, Louise, at the general manager's request. I had extensive experience in retail, and it was hoped I could influence them

to try and get some changes from their corporate offices.

As I approached the store, I looked at it from a customer's perspective. A store looks much different from halfway down the mall as opposed to standing in front of it. A store such as Karl's, located in a corner or pop-out position, should pay close attention to this aspect.

Upon entering the store, I found the store manager just finishing up a floor move. It was a summer season, and she had placed some very bright colors up towards the front of her store. She was very excited about the changes she and her district manager had just made. When she asked what I thought about her store, I told her that from the front of her store it looked great. However, from down the mall it was a different story. A customer would see it from a different viewpoint, and wouldn't necessarily be excited with what they saw. She was both amazed and confused.

Then she asked me to explain what I meant. I explained to her that the perspective of her store is changed dramatically once you step outside of it. When you walk away from your store down the hallway and then turn around and look at it again, what do you see? She wasn't sure.

I pulled her to the front of her store, told her to look down the hallway and describe what she saw. About eight stores away was a shoe store. It also had a popout storefront. From where she stood Edna could see a huge sale sign, along with neat rows of the same style shoe in different colors, displayed along the wall. After she described what she saw, I asked her to look further at the display and tell me what she was looking at.

Not quite catching my drift, I explained to her she was looking at a tremendous impact of goods. Not only did you see that there is a sale going on in that store and maybe I should go down there and see what they have on sale, but you can also see from the variety of shoes that they carry that maybe I will find something in the store suitable for me.

I walked her down the mall to the shoe store, turned her around to look at her own store, and asked her to describe what she saw. She was amazed! Amazed at the difference from what she saw standing in front of her store, to what the customer at this end of the mall was going to see. "What do you see?" I asked her. "I see a blouse" she said. The gears were now in motion. She went on to say that some of the merchandise made no sense when looked at from this angle. For instance, she had placed all bright colors in the front of the store. On a front tee stand there were some white dresses. Looking at it from this angle, what she could see didn't go with the rest of her theme.

As we proceeded to walk closer to her store, we stopped again and she described what she saw. The closer she got, the wider the angle of vision, the more merchandise came into view. She realized that the way she had displayed her goods, made her store appear to not have any (or very much) merchandise.

Once again, I stressed to her the story her store needed to tell. When the customer is down at the other side of the mall, something in that storefront should tell her "Hey, I'm interesting, come in and visit me." If you don't do it, the customer isn't going to come into your store, and you've missed a potential sale.

As we walked down the mall, we discussed the various stores, their front windows, or front displays. Not just clothing stores, but shoe stores, and book stores as well. We discussed what kind of an impact they were making with their merchandise. Neatness, orderliness, the colors they used, large photo posters, sale signs, all these things were being combined in different ways to tell their own particular story inviting the customer to come in.

Once again I emphasized that you must look at your store from a customer's perspective, you've got to walk down the mall and see your store as your customer sees it, and make adjustments accordingly. Ask yourself, "What makes me want to go into my store?"

Edna returned to her store, determined to make changes. I reviewed with her district manager, the things we had discussed. They later took pictures of their storefront, sent them to their corporate offices requesting the items we had asked for. They remerchandised their storefront, changed several displays, created an impact with their goods, and ended up with a much more appealing storefront, which resulted in increased sales. Six months later, new carpet and paint arrived!

This story best sums up why an attractive storefront is so vital to your store's overall appeal - it can be the difference between a customer or no customer. A sale or no sale.

## YOUR CUSTOMER - KEEPING THEIR INTEREST

Since we've already discussed how to provide excellent customer service, I'm not going to review it again here. Once you get a customer into your store, you need to make sure you are providing excellent service.

On some occasions the merchandise will be left to present itself. This may occur for any one of the following reasons: during busier seasons; at certain times of the day; perhaps you had to step away to answer the phone; or when the customer prefers to wait on him or herself. Whatever the reason, it's essential to pay maximum attention to your presentation. Whether that presentation is your store as a whole, or a particular area of your store, it could be the difference between holding your customer's attention until you return, or a customer walking away.

There are several types of interior displays. One is readily accessible to your customer. This could be either a tabletop or rack front display. The inaccessible display is generally due to its expense, such as fine jewelry; or its fragileness, such as china. This display will require assistance from the salesperson when a desired piece is found and needs further examination.

In both types of interior displays, attracting attention to the merchandise is the key to promoting sales. This is another area where signage can play an important role. Whether it's to help you find the merchandise, learn the price, give quality information such as care, sizes available, etc., or just to create an image, signs which fail to relay information about the merchandise, fail in their primary mission.

When presenting merchandise to your customer, it's important for that merchandise to be presented together and in some type of uniformity. That is, from the smallest to the largest, etc. The following story is one example of presentation.

> A housewares store had experienced very weak sales for quite some time. While visiting the store, at the manager's request, I noticed lots of things that were improper or made no sense. The manager had been trying to come up with some innovative displays that would help sell his merchandise, and he wanted to know some of my ideas since he was experiencing what every manager does at one time or another - mental block. First, I told him that a good way to alleviate this mental block was to visit another store with similar merchandise to get some fresh ideas. Steal them, implement them to your own standards, but do something! If it works, if it sells, your overall sales will increase. Most importantly, customers will continue to come back.

In talking with the manager, about things which made no sense, I pointed out an area of the store where the wicker furniture was displayed. I made the statement if the customer cannot picture this item in his or her home, if the customer has no perceived idea of how this item will be useful to him the customer is not going to buy it!

I pointed out that both white and natural wicker were mixed together. Also, because the wicker pieces were piled on top of each other, it was hard to tell what went with what, or for that matter, what you were even looking at.

I asked the manager that if he were a customer coming to buy wicker furniture, would he be putting white and natural in the same room? The answer was obviously no. Then I asked him why it was displayed that way. If it doesn't make sense to the customer, why would the customer want to buy it? We proceeded to put like items together, creating minirooms or areas of wicker pieces that tied in together - hopefully to create multiple sales. It worked. Sales did increase!

There were several other things I noticed. The store was extremely dusty. Not exactly a pleasant experience for a customer who handles a piece of merchandise, then lays it down only to discover their hands are covered in dust! It's very important to keep your store clean.

One final point, make things easy for your customer to find. Don't have like items separated throughout various shelves, throughout your store, etc. Keep like items together. If you're selling denim, keep the denim together. It's fine to separate fashion denim from basic denim, or even men's denim from women's denim. But keep the basics together in one area. Don't have some on one rack, and some across the store, and some in the back. Make it easy for the customer to find. Make it easy for the customer to shop. Make it an enjoyable experience for them, and the customer will return!

Handling multiple customers requires courtesy, energy, and knowledge of your store and its merchandise. It's similar to cooking dinner in a way; having the roast in the oven, cooking the vegetables on the stove and preparing the salad all at the same time. It is, in fact a matter of timing too. You're not going to leave a customer in the middle of a question about a purchase, nor do you leave a pot to boil over.

It's important to let your customer know what you're up to. Ever been in a dressing room trying on clothes, chatting away and upon opening the door, find there's nobody there? Makes you feel pretty silly doesn't it? There's nothing more aggravating than being half-dressed, realizing you need a different size, only to discover you're stranded because your salesperson has left and you don't know where to. So what do you do? Get dressed again and find it yourself, or do you stay put and hope the salesperson will return before you catch pneumonia?

The golden rule applies here, treat your customers the way you would wish to be treated if you were in their shoes. When you need to step away, tell them, or better yet, ask them. "Would you excuse me for a moment? I'll be right back." "Would it be alright if I let you look for a minute while I go help this other customer?" By asking the customer's permission, you not only avoid alienating them, you make them feel important. Just don't forget to return every few minutes to find out how they're doing, answer any questions, or give further assistance.

Handling multiple customers rules can apply to several instances. For instance, the back door rings and your shipment of 50 cases has just arrived and you need to check it in, or the telephone rings and it's a company conference call. In either case don't forget your customer. They are, after all, the reason you're there.

If necessary, get another salesperson to help you. Explain to your customer the situation. "Mrs. Jones, I'm sorry but there's a phone call I need to take. John here is going to help you until I can return." The extra courtesy will go a long way. Don't forget to introduce them to the salesperson - it's a nice touch.

If another salesperson isn't available, you must learn that your first priority is to the customer. Nothing is more important! Tell the caller your situation, hopefully they can call back. Tell the driver of the truck to please be patient while you do multiple handstands between him and the customer. They're much more likely to be patient with an explanation.

Since we're somewhat on the subject of phones anyway, let's digress for a minute and discuss proper phone etiquette. How many times have you called a place of business and had someone answer the phone and not understood a word they've said? Make sure when you or your associates answer the phone they speak in a clear and concise manner. "Good morning, Byron's Gifts!" Some stores want you to introduce yourself as well, "Good morning, Harry's Auto Parts. This is Jack speaking!" Several companies like to use the phone answering process to relay special information about a sale or new merchandise. "Good afternoon, Joanne's, all our sweaters are 30% off this week!" "Sandy's Shoes, all our winter boots have just arrived!"

Remember to be polite. Smile when you answer the phone, you sound more pleasant. Be enthusiastic! Don't sound like you just got out of bed. If you're extremely busy, don't be afraid to ask the caller to call back. Most would prefer this to being placed on hold forever anyway! However, it's generally best to help them right away. Always try to answer the phone within three rings. Neither the caller nor the people in your store like to hear the incessant ringing of a phone.

As customers come in all shapes and sizes, so do they also arrive in different moods.

Handling an angry customer takes a bit of finesse and patience, along with an even temper. Remember, smile. Be courteous. These are generally the best ways to disarm an angry customer. If proper steps are taken, an angry customer can become a satisfied customer, or at the very least, a calm one. If there are other customers in the store, try to get your problem customer in a more remote area to avoid upsetting other shoppers. It's very important to listen carefully to what your customer says as he/she explains why they're upset. Repeat what they say to ensure you both understand the problem. The object to understanding the complaint is to resolve it. One can not be done without the other. "Let me make sure I understand what you're saying, you washed the blouse per the instructions and it no longer fits?" Or perhaps "A salesperson told you that you could return this item and get your money back?"

Many situations will arise where handling the problem to your customer's satisfaction may depend upon company policy. A customer demanding a refund, when the store policy is to give credits only, will require firm resolve on your part. At this point, explain what the store policy is concerning returns. Apologize to the customer for any inconvenience this will cause them. On occasion, hopefully they will be few, the customer will demand a higher chain of command. Don't take offense to this, many times the squeaky wheel gets the grease and they know this. Often, when they go over your head they will, in fact, get what they want. Don't be upset, you've done your job. You have followed policy as you were hired to do. Give them the name and <u>business</u> phone number or address where your supervisor can be reached during working hours. (With your supervisor's prior approval of course.) Again, be pleasant. It might be a good idea to ask for the customer's name. Explain that you will be making a report about the problem and will be forwarding it on to your supervisor. It's a good idea to keep a file of any problems you may have encountered. When it's time for an explanation, you'll have all the facts written down in front of you. It's amazing the important things you may forget over a period of time. If it were to come up in your review, you don't want important details left out.

When enough is enough. There will be occasions when a customer becomes so loud, so abusive and so out of hand that it's best to ask them to leave. This is in an extreme situation, and should be handled with caution. There will be times when you can't help the customer with their problem due to store policy or another reason. If the situation is such, and you've tried to explain calmly to the customer and the abuse continues, the only thing remaining is to tell the customer he/she must leave the store.

There are occasions when someone simply comes in to hassle you or your salespeople. Jealous boyfriends, angry parents, or some obnoxious male trying to pick up a girl, are all situations which should be handled delicately but firmly.

Another scenario may be a customer whose credit card is not approved on a particular sale. This generally is an embarrassing ordeal for a customer. Don't aggravate the situation by assuming the customer is over their limit, or hasn't paid their bill, and certainly don't tell them this! Follow the instructions of the credit card company. They may wish to speak with the customer and may ask you to retain the card and mail it back to them. Depending on your own company policy, do what they tell you. You may get a reward if the card is found to be stolen. Explain what you're doing to the customer, tell them if they have any questions, to call the bank issuing the card and find out from them the reason. Don't make a big ordeal of this. Speak quietly both to the customer and when calling the credit card company. The better you handle this type of situation, the less trouble in the end from both the customer and your supervisor.

## YOUR CUSTOMER - KEEPING THEM LOYAL

Keeping the customer coming back to your store can be accomplished in several ways, most of which have already been discussed. Key items such as an attractive store, good customer service, ease of locating merchandise and cleanliness are all essential parts of everyday business. A liberal return policy is very important, especially during the holiday season. It's imperative these days to stand behind your merchandise even if the manufacturer won't. All these things reflect the personality of your store. That is, what the customer perceives as the benefit your store offers. Obviously the more benefits perceived, the greater chance of beating out the competition, and the greater your sales volume. Reminding customers of these benefits can be accomplished through advertising.

After the sale, repair any damage or disarray left behind from your previous customers. This includes hanging up any garments so they will appear fresh and ready for your next customer. Any items removed from display should be returned or replaced. On many occasions an entire display will be purchased, in which case it will be necessary to replace the display with another one to continue with the store's continuity.

Don't wait until the end of the day to put your store back in order if business is fairly slow. After all, if one display is sold, another one could be. Remember the impulse buying rule? (Two thirds of all buying decisions are made while in your store.)

A customer card file is an extra selling tool many stores have incorporated as part of their customer service program. The information listed includes name, address, phone number, sizes, etc. It may also include information such as brand of clothing preferred, and style of clothing preferred. Dates of visits and/or purchases, even birthdays are listed. Separate cards for each family member should be on file.

If a customer card file is kept, it will be necessary to update it. List the items purchased or needed. If a minimum purchase is made, perhaps a quick thank you can be written down on a post card. It's best to do this while it's still fresh in your mind. This is always a great way to impress a customer and let them know how much you appreciate their business.

Keeping the customer loyal to your store is possible by providing both on the scene and behind the scene satisfaction of their needs. In lieu of this, it's important to know what your competition is doing to combat the situation.

## THE COMPETITION - WHAT ARE THEY DOING?

"The only difference between stores is the way they treat their customers." This is becoming more and more true these days, especially with all the acquisitions and mergers. It is said there's not much difference between a sweater from The Limited, Lerner or Limited Express. Many stores are copying each other in style, layout, merchandise, etc. It's getting tougher and tougher staying ahead of the competition. However, it's not an impossible task. Trends may change daily and it's important to stay on top of your industry. If you aren't giving the customer what they want, they'll go elsewhere.

So you may ask, how do you do it? One way is to read, read, read! There are dozens of various business magazines, books, articles, etc., to keep you abreast of the changing times. More importantly, who's changing with them. Nordstrom is a department store chain based out of Seattle. It is highly respected first and foremost (and sometimes highly feared by others) because it is renowned for its outstanding customer service. People shop there for this reason alone. The Limited, the top selling sportswear chain in the nation, consists of: The Limited, Lerner New York, Structure, Lane Bryant, Victoria's Secret, Limited Express, Limited Too, and more. It's well known for its quick response in inventory turn around time. Les Wexner, their president, is considered by some no less than a genius. Toys 'R Us - a super toy store, and Home Depot - a home improvement chain, are known for being category killers. That is, if they don't have it, you won't find it. Nor will you find it for less. Anyone in retailing who isn't familiar with these companies, should be. They are considered to be the leaders in the industry. This being the case, you should be familiar with what they're doing and how they're doing it!

The number one key is awareness on a regular basis. Do you know what the competition is even doing? Do you know who they are? How do stores on a local basis compare to you in advertising, sales, merchandise, displays, and salespeople? You should be taking a look at each of these aspects on a regular basis.

First, consider their advertising, and ask yourself these questions:

- "Are they running a sale?"
- "Are they using catchy phrases, jingles, or logos?"
- "How do their ads look compared to ours?"
- "Can ours be improved?"

Viewing newspapers and magazines, as well as other mediums will give you a hands on grasp of what their advertising looks like.

Next, ask yourself, "How do their sales compare with mine?" You should be comparing not only on a dollar per square foot basis, but a dollar per dollar basis as well. (Many of these figures can be obtained from your mall office or downtown merchants association.) You should compare yourself to others in your category - whether it's apparel or services, and compare yourself to national figures too. Annual sales figures can be obtained from the ULI Dollars and Cents of Shopping Centers, as well as the Newspapers Ad Bureaus Planbook.

You should be taking time out to visit other stores and see what they're doing. Once again you should be noting the following:

- How are the competition's prices compared to yours?
- Do they have similar or the same merchandise on sale?

- Are you adjusting your prices to either match or beat theirs?
- If you don't have the authority to do so, are you at least informing upper management of the variances?
- How similar/different is their merchandise?
- Do they have a special niche that you should explore?
- Are their displays more creative or effective in selling merchandise?
- What does their signage look like?
- Can some of their ideas be applied in your store?
- Do they carry a fuller line of similar or the same goods?
- How well are their salespeople trained?
- Do they know the answers to your questions?
- Do they close early?
- Are they rude to last minute shoppers?

The list is endless of good questions to ask yourself, but more importantly, you must answer them as well. Finding out the answers isn't worthwhile unless you implement the changes necessary. Apply these ideas to your own situation to stay ahead of your competition.

One option is to serve smaller segments of the market that are under-serviced by larger stores. Many 'accessory only' stores have appeared to take up one such segment or niche. Victoria's Secret has many advantages over a lingerie department in a department store. Whether you will offer a service or a specific type of merchandise, this niche finding has been a tried and true factor, especially in today's market. Most noticeably by declining sales of many department stores, and increasing sales of stores such as The Limited, The Gap and Toys 'R Us.

Be different from your competition. It's the only way you will have a chance to stand out in the crowd. Whether your difference lies in customer service, merchandise or display, it's important that you remain flexible. Quick changes may be necessary and it's important to be open to them. Teach your people to embrace change.

I've often heard managers get upset when change is necessary, wondering why, refusing to be cooperative, and hearing the age old phrase "But we've always done it this way!" Thoroughly explain the reasons why you want the change. This will usually help reduce the negativism. Then, follow through on the changes made to determine whether they helped or not. Make the necessary adjustments to ensure more customer awareness of your store, this will help lead to increased sales.

## THE COMPETITION - AVOIDING TUNNEL VISION

Once you see your store from your customer's perspective, you will become aware of many things you might have been tuning out. My favorite terminology for this is to "Take off your blinders".

Many of us get stuck in a rut and don't even realize it. We become so used to doing things a certain way that we lose sight - or put on blinders, to the changes going on around us.

For instance, how often do you take a different approach? How many times do you walk, drive to work, or enter a place of business from another direction, to obtain a different perspective?

I challenge you to try it! Park on the other side of the mall or down a different street. Generally you'll discover something you never noticed before but that has been there, or been changed for quite some time.

Keeping up with the competition, or staying ahead of them, is a constant battle. By increasing your awareness, remaining flexible in a constantly changing environment, and capitalizing on your differences, the battle between you and your competition can be won!

# 4

# ADVERTISING

## ADVERTISING - WHY YOU SHOULD

"You have to spend money to make money" is an old but appropriate saying when it comes to advertising. Too many smaller retailers ride on the skirts of the larger stores in malls, strip centers and even downtown areas. Granted, larger stores have a larger ad budget, but smaller merchants need to advertise as well.

There are many reasons to advertise for your store. Perhaps you're new, or have just relocated, or maybe you have a new look due to a renovation. You may want to distinguish yourself from the competition by a unique slogan. Making a fashion statement during peak or non-peak selling periods is another reason. Promoting an event such as a cooking demonstration or a sale is another.

Whatever the reason, the ad program should be tailored to your own needs.

## ADVERTISING - HOW TO

There are two types of advertising, institutional and promotional. Institutional advertising is used to project an overall image rather than to sell a specific item. Promotional advertising is used to promote specific items.

When developing an ad, there are several things to keep in mind. First and foremost, any ad produced should capture attention. You should devise a logo for your store and use it in every ad. This helps to make your store ad easily recognizable. Obviously this doesn't apply to a radio ad. However if a slogan or jingle is part of the logo, it should be incorporated in your radio ad. Second, your store location and possibly even store hours should be listed. Third, make sure the ad is believable. Fourth, the ad should convince the store's target customer to shop the sponsoring store rather than the competition. All these concepts should apply to each and every ad whether you use print or electronic media.

The types of advertising most common to retailing are as follows: newspaper, radio, television, outdoor, direct mail, and magazines. There are advantages and disadvantages to each. However, before you determine which medium you will use, you must first determine your advertising budget.

In developing your ad budget there are certain factors to keep in mind. First, it will be necessary to develop your budget in relation to need. Although the industry average is to base the budget on three to five percent of net sales, you may find you need to spend more. This may be due to location in a low traffic or problem area, recent construction, etc. You might wish to determine your budget based on seasonal sales goals. These goals may be based on past performance.

Second, you will also want to develop your budget over a certain period of time to allow for continuous coverage in addition to special sales or promotions.

Third, you want to have some built in flexibility.

Once your overall budget has been determined, you will need to decide which and how much media to buy. You may decide to buy 100% newspaper, or perhaps 50% newspaper and 50% radio. Perhaps the ratio will be 60/40. Before deciding which media to use, you must first determine who, when, where, how often and in what way you want to reach your customer. Who your customer is can be determined by their demographics, life-styles, or attitudes. Demographics such as age, income, education, occupation, etc., should be specific. When to reach your customer may be determined by the product. For example, if you sell swimwear, Spring and Summer are your primary seasons. Where does your customer live? In the city or suburb? How many ad messages will be necessary before a sale can be made? In what environment do you want to reach your customer? Your customer might be less educated and watches more television. Perhaps tourists are a big percentage and outdoor billboards are most important. Remember to keep a close eye on what your competitor is doing. We can learn a lot by watching others. Remember, advertising works. If you find it's not working for you, perhaps it's time to reassess how you advertise. It's also important to keep in mind that advertising is only as good as the product you sell. All the advertising in the world will not get a customer to buy if your merchandise is neither desired, nor any good.

Newspapers are considered the top advertising medium. It is a flexible medium in that the size of the ad can vary and the copy can be detailed or general. It gets fast results. The ad can be placed very close to lead time or deadline. Generally the coverage is wide, yet the circulation is aimed at a compact geographical area. A newspaper's disadvantage is it is here today - gone tomorrow, and so is your ad.

Keeping a file or scrapbook of your favorite ads can become helpful when designing or creating your own. Although you can't copy the ad exactly, the general concept or idea may be repeated. There are even resources available such as the United States Institute of Marketing in Oakmont, Pennsylvania that compile some of the best ads nationwide.

Don't squander your money on small ads. It's better to use sizable ads that command attention. Spend money on good artwork. In fashion ads, approximately 85% of the ad's effectiveness is based on how arresting the artwork is to the eye.

Adding color to your ads is also likely to add awareness of the item.

Use the following tips when creating your ad. Ads with good copy - what you want to say; artwork - your photos or graphics; layout - the way your ad is arranged, are more likely to be read. Keep the ad simple. It should be easy to read from a layout standpoint as well as verbiage. Clutter and difficult or technical words should be avoided. Complete sentences are often easier to read than phrases or words. Be specific, list sizes, and colors available. Include the price. Create a sense of urgency to buy now! Create a sale ad that will produce a return of ten times your investment. That is, a $20 ad will produce $200 in sales.

Co-op advertising is advertising shared with your manufacturer/supplier, both in space and dollars. It can increase your ad dollars by a significant amount. There are several different types of co-op advertising: traditional, promotional allowance, and dealer support. The Newspaper Advertising Bureau's Retail Co-op Recovery program can take the hassle out of dealing with co-op ads. (This is certainly not the only source, however. Check with your radio and television stations as well). Co-op ads can be simple and should certainly be taken advantage of.

Radio advertising is cost efficient. Radio is an excellent way to support newspaper ads. The combination of both, adds to greater awareness. Radio production is generally less expensive than other mediums. Unlike newspaper, no other message is run simultaneous - that is, at least on the same station. Radio has a here and now quality, and produces quick results. Its greatest disadvantage is that once heard, the message is gone and can't be replayed or reviewed. Thus, with radio, repetition of an ad is a must. In selecting your station, several points should be taken into consideration. Does the radio station's format match your own store's image? Who listens to the station? How large is its audience? Who else advertises on the station? Are the rates reasonable and can they fit within your budget?

How do you compute the difference between two similar stations? First, you must determine the reach. That is, the number of different people that will hear your ad at least once in a given time period. Then you must determine what your frequency will be, or the average number of times an individual listener will hear the commercial. The number of gross impressions resulting (reach times frequency) will determine which station you should select.

Follow this example, remember, as reach increases, frequency decreases:

Station ABC has a reach of 10,000 and costs $25 per 30 second ad. If you have $500 in your budget, your gross impressions will be 200,000.
$500/$25 is 20 (number of ads you can afford to run)
10,000 (reach) x 20 (frequency) = 200,000 (gross impressions)

Station DEF has a reach of 25,000 and costs $40 per 30 second ad. If you still have $500 in your budget your gross impressions will be 300,000
$500/$40 = 12.5 (The number of ads you can afford to run is 12, since you can't run half an ad. This means you would actually spend $480)
25,000 (reach) x 12 (frequency) = 300,000 (gross impressions)

Since DEF has a greater number of gross impressions, you would place your ads on this station. Again, this assumes all else is equal.

The copy for a radio ad should be clear, concise and focused on customer benefits. The store name should be mentioned several times and the location should also be included. The ad should be written using attention getting phrases. Sound effects or a jingle make both the ad and the store more recognizable. Although 10, 30, and 60 second spots are generally available for radio ads, 30 seconds is the most common length of time. Make sure whoever does the voice on your ads has speech that is not heavily accented and that their words are easily understood. Some stations will write and produce your ad for free. That is, it is included in the placement cost. Some stations charge extra. Be sure you know which one will do what before you give the go-ahead.

More and more people are entertaining at home. Positioning or placing an advertisement in a more relaxed atmosphere such as the home, can be a great advantage. Television is one excellent medium in which this can be done. Television adds color, and unlike print is three dimensional. It adds motion. It reaches a wider variety of customers. It can talk to the viewer one on one. It is more attention getting. It can be an advantage over newspaper and/or radio when demonstrating the function of a product is necessary. Your message will be delivered in a more relaxed atmosphere. Television however, generally is expensive, both in airtime and production.

Network television consists of NBC, ABC, CBS and FOX. Network television - which is currently more widely watched than cable, (although cable is right on its heels) is also considerably more expensive. It therefore, has more national advertisers such as beer and car ads as opposed to a local Mom and Pop store. There are 250 markets for television throughout the country. Larger markets such as Los Angeles will cost more than say a market in West Virginia. However, it is less expensive per thousand people. This is again because there is a greater viewing audience in LA.

Cable television which includes: CNN, USA, ESPN, Lifetime, etc., is generally more locally oriented. It can be as inexpensive as some radio advertising but its viewing audience may be very small.

Independently programmed stations are also a viable option. They are usually less expensive than network but more so than cable. Again check your cost per thousand to determine your most efficient buy. Movies and sports are usually the programs aired on these stations.

Keep in mind that many households (over 50%) own video recorders. This can mean that although the program you specified to place an advertisement on might be watched, your commercial may not be seen due to that infamous 'fast forward' button.

Producing a television commercial requires good forethought and planning. A story board is a segmented diagram of what will be featured for each scene in the ad. It also includes dialogue written under each scene. If displays are part of the ad, make sure they are clean, neat and orderly. Make sure lighting is sufficient. Generally it's better to add additional lighting if inside to insure a clearer picture. This is especially true if you are trying to feature detail, such as links in a necklace. The voice on an ad can be produced 'live' in the store or dubbed on to the commercial in-house.

Many stations will have special electronic equipment such as an abacus that will produce special effects. This may include lettering across a screen or a page turning effect. Check with your local station or your agency to find out what's available, before you're ready to actually produce an ad. Some of the biggest mistakes local retailers make is in being unprepared for the production portion. Come prepared to discuss your ideas. Listen to the experts! They know what can and cannot be done. Your grandiose ideas may be impossible to do on a local level and/or just too expensive. Again, listen to the experts to determine what may best suit your needs. The Television Advertising Bureau, Inc. in New York City (212-486-1111) has many tips to help you create an effective ad. Whether it's producing an ad or establishing a store image, your local television station should have access to this information.

Outdoor advertising can be an effective medium. Location is the key. Whether you're on the left or right hand side, be sure your billboard is highly visible. Look out for trees in the area. Some states have laws that don't allow you to cut them down if they grow up and cover your message. So be aware! Check out the site before you sign a contract.

When advertising outdoors, be sure to keep the message simple and short. The average number of words that will be read on a billboard on the highway while traveling at high speeds, is eight. If the billboard is at a traffic light, however, more time to read would allow for more words to be added. But don't get carried away! The aim is to catch the viewer's eye with a few powerful words. Color is another good way to attract attention. Black on yellow is the most readable. Stick with primary colors when possible. Neon colors are becoming popular and increase visibility and impact. However, you want to differentiate yourself from your neighbor's board. Especially if you are sharing a board. If they've used these colors already, make sure you select contrasting ones. You obviously want your message to stand out.

The great thing about billboards is their flexibility. They work all day, every day, and even at night. They reach all kinds of people. However, on the flip side, there is a lack of audience selectivity. If there are a barrage of billboards on the highway, yours may be missed. The cost of a billboard will vary whether its location is on the left or right side of the road, whether or not it's lighted, how many people will see it, and how often changes will need to be made. Generally, due to a substantial reach and frequency, it's a good investment.

There are many types of outdoor advertising. Beginning with the most common - billboards, to the more uncommon - behind the back of a plane. (Anyone who's been to Daytona Beach, Florida has seen these.) There are signs on park benches, backs of taxicabs and busses. There are signs inside subway cars as well. Many of the tips listed above can apply to all these types of advertising.

Buying at home has become increasingly popular over the last several years. People find they are inundated with catalogs - which have become extremely popular. One advantage of direct mail is the personal contact it allows you to have with your customer. The one to one communication piece viewed in the privacy of the home can be very effective in making a sale. Many direct mail pieces allow the customer to either make a purchase over the phone or mail in an order.

Department stores and some specialty retailers spend an average of five percent on direct mail. One great thing about direct mail is not only can you select the coverage and be as specific as you want, but the piece you send can be anything from a postcard to a full blown catalog. This flexibility is important especially when you consider the cost of mailing, let alone the cost of production of your piece. Whether it's an insert in the monthly billing of your charge customer, or a tabloid from the local mall, keep in mind the average response rate for any direct mail piece is only one to three percent. You might find it will be too cost prohibitive for your budget.

Convenience is becoming more and more important in the time, or lack of time, driven world as we know it today. Telling the customer of a sale or a new arrival of goods is certainly important. Hopefully, it will create a sense of urgency to place the order or come in for a visit and make a purchase. There should always be a perceived benefit to your mail piece. In other words, what's in it for them? Are you saving them time, money, or both? Are they going to get an extra gift or bonus if they act now? Is it merely information you are disbursing? You want whatever you send to stand out from the 'junk mail'.

Some advertisers consider magazines a form of direct mail, although it would depend on the type. Depending on the content of the magazine and whether it's a weekly, monthly, or quarterly, your ad will be seen time and again by many people. Magazines offer a very select audience, and are considered to be the best medium to reach a specific target audience. Ads may vary in size from 1/8, 1/4, 1/2 or a full page. Many of the same rules apply to both magazine ads and newspaper ads, such as adding color for greater effectiveness. Color in magazines is much truer to the real thing. However, with magazines, most ads are more institutional in nature. Although the audience may be more selective, the cost also is generally more.

Another way for the public to find out about your store is in the form of a press release. A press release is not an advertisement, it is news and should be treated as such. This news about your store comes in a variety of ways: perhaps you are donating to charity or working with the community on a particular project; your store might have an upcoming anniversary that you wish to announce; a relocation or remodeling are also newsworthy items. It's important to include basic facts about your store: name, location, etc.

The publicity you receive via a press release will help to key into the local citizens minds that you are a solid member in good standing with the community. Another advantage is that is doesn't cost you a thing!

## ADVERTISING - PROMOTIONS

Promotions go hand in hand with advertising. Generally they don't cost you anything but time and a little effort. The events I'm talking about range from fashion shows to your center newsletter. When most malls put on a fashion show, they provide everything but the clothing and props. If you operate a fashion apparel store you should definitely jump on the band wagon. It's a great way for the public to see your merchandise. Though it may not result in immediate sales, it gives the customer a good 'feel' of what your merchandise is all about.

Non-apparel stores can find ways their merchandise can fit in for props. Whether it's books for a Back-to-School show, or puppies to present warm and cuddly overcoats in autumn, every store can be tied together in some manner. Glasses for models from the vision stores, background props from the furniture store. These are just a few ideas possible to use. Stretch your imagination and see just how far it can go.

Many malls have their own fashion or teen board. If their models don't fit your clientele, ask if you can provide your own models. Providing your models show up for rehearsals, this may be a good alternative to avoiding shows altogether. If this isn't a possibility, you should consider presenting your own show. Most local models, especially inexperienced ones, work for free. It's fun, and a personal kick for them. Even some of the smallest towns have businesses that can provide a microphone and sound system. All that's left is : to pick out the music, merchandise, time and place, a theme for the show, props, and how you want the choreography of the show to run. Whew, sound like a lot? It is, but it can be a lot of fun.

An alternative to fashion shows is 'tea room modeling'. Effectively, this requires that you work with a local restaurant to let them allow models to show off your merchandise. Models would stop off at select tables, (not every one - it becomes too redundant if you do this!) show merchandise, talk about its features, price, where to buy, etc. Sometimes merchandise is sold on the spot! Tea room modeling can occur once a month or once a week, depending on how much time you have to plan. It usually works best during lunch. Many restauranteurs feel it's an added draw for a lunch crowd to see the latest fashions and won't charge. If you do advertise, be sure to inform the restaurant their name will be included. It's another incentive for them to cooperate.

Giving fellow mall or strip center employees a 10% discount on regular priced merchandise is a terrific way to get business for a small price on your part.

Participating in mall or strip center events is one way to get your name known to fellow tenants. They could be potential customers. If free advertising is offered by the center because of a special category event, TAKE IT! I was constantly amazed by the lack of participation of some stores even though free things were offered. No company should be <u>that</u> inflexible.

Display windows in empty storefronts can be a great way to expand your store's visibility. Check with management about their policies. Most companies would prefer an attractive window to an untold sign of a store that went out of business. Perhaps you and other stores can rotate its usage for free.

Newsletters are a good way of letting fellow tenants know of special events, promotions of store personnel, etc. A little effort on your part to contact the office responsible goes a long way. Not only does it show others you're on the ball, but also, employees will love seeing their name in print and will appreciate the fact that you were responsible for it.

There are many ways to get your name in front of the public's eye. Most of them can be yours for the taking if you just inquire. Don't let these opportunities slip away due to your laziness or disorganization. See these opportunities for what they are - a free means of advertising for your store. Take advantage of them!

# 5

# APPENDIX

## TIME MANAGEMENT
## CASE STUDY

It's Monday morning, 8:30 am. How would you rate the following maintenance list left by your DM over the weekend, of things to accomplish by the end of the month?

| | Priority high/low | Value high/low |
|---|---|---|
| Clean cash wrap | | |
| Clean bathroom | | |
| Replace light bulbs/fixtures | | |
| Organize back room | | |
| Fill-in missing displays | | |
| Organize bags/boxes at cash wrap | | |
| Dust and clean register | | |
| Organize hanger bins | | |
| File paperwork | | |
| Clean store sign | | |
| Dust and clean fixtures | | |
| Sweep and mop back room | | |
| Steam clean carpets | | |
| Clean trash can thoroughly | | |
| Clean mannequins, check for loose parts | | |

Which items can be delegated?
Which items should be completed today?
Which items should be completed by the end of the week?

# TIME MANAGEMENT
## CASE STUDY

| | Priority high/low | Value high/low |
|---|---|---|
| Clean cash wrap | high | high |
| Clean bathroom | high | low |
| Replace light bulbs/fixtures | high | high |
| Organize back room | high | low |
| Fill-in missing displays | high | high |
| Organize bags/ boxes at cash wrap | high | low |
| Dust and clean register | high | high |
| Organize hanger bins | high | low |
| File paperwork | high | high |
| Clean store sign | low | low |
| Dust and clean fixtures | low | high |
| Sweep and mop back room | high/low | low |
| Steam clean carpets | low | low |
| Clean trash can thoroughly | low | low |
| Clean mannequins, check for loose parts | high | high |

Which items can be delegated? All but the paperwork.
Which items should be completed today? Anything ranking high - high.
Which items should be completed by the end of the week? Anything ranking high - low.

*Please note, your own rankings may differ slightly based on your own perceptions of what is a high/low priority and value.

## SCHEDULING

Employee work schedules if made on a regular basis will avoid unnecessary changes. Time off should be asked for well in advance, and should be designated on a first come, first serve basis.

Daily and weekly schedules will help to insure that tasks are handled on a timely basis. Assign the various responsibilities to employees to insure their completion by the day's end.

When filling out the weekly/daily schedules, try to insure the following:

1. Fill out sales goals; LY, TY - plan and actual. This will keep you informed of where you stand, how far to go, etc.
2. Fill out the percent of daily business that must be reached for your sales goal.
3. List anything happening in the mall/center which may affect daily business.
4. Fill out when breaks and lunches are to occur. This will help insure proper floor coverage.
5. Make note of any irregularities in the schedule. For example: large shipments requiring extra people, training hours, special hours/ sales, etc.

YOUR STORE SCHEDULE Week Ending Date_________

| Employee<br>Name | Sunday<br>LY$<br>Plan $<br>TY$<br>Comments: | Monday<br>LY$<br>Plan $<br>TY$ | Tuesday<br>LY$<br>Plan $<br>TY$ | Wednesday<br>LY$<br>Plan $<br>TY$ | Thursday<br>LY$<br>Plan $<br>TY$ | Friday<br>LY$<br>Plan $<br>TY$ | Saturday<br>LY$<br>Plan $<br>TY$ | TOTAL<br>LY$<br>Plan $<br>TY$ |
|---|---|---|---|---|---|---|---|---|
| | | | | | | | | |
| | | | | | | | | |
| | | | | | | | | |
| | | | | | | | | |
| | | | | | | | | |
| Total<br>Schedule Hrs | | | | | | | | |
| Total<br>Actual Hrs | | | | | | | | |
| Benefit/<br>Trainee Hrs | | | | | | | | |
| Total Hrs<br>Paid/Overtime | | | | | | | | |

## TRAINING CHECKLIST

| NAME | Sales Training | Store Tour | Dress Code | Floor Coverage | Suggestive Selling | Sales Goals | Fitting Room Procedure | Multiple Customers | Product Knowledge | Loss Prevention | Processing Shipment | Backstock Rotation | Store Maintenance | Closing Procedures | Sales Contests | Item of The Day |
|---|---|---|---|---|---|---|---|---|---|---|---|---|---|---|---|---|
| | | | | | | | | | | | | | | | | |
| | | | | | | | | | | | | | | | | |
| | | | | | | | | | | | | | | | | |
| | | | | | | | | | | | | | | | | |
| | | | | | | | | | | | | | | | | |
| | | | | | | | | | | | | | | | | |
| | | | | | | | | | | | | | | | | |
| | | | | | | | | | | | | | | | | |
| | | | | | | | | | | | | | | | | |
| | | | | | | | | | | | | | | | | |

Sample maintenance checklist...

## BACK ROOM ORGANIZATION

_____Make sure all back stock is organized; by style, color, etc.

_____Organize and update all layaways. Return any overdue ones to the sales floor.

_____Separate and store all hangers by style, color, and size as follows:

1. Dress hangers
2. Pant hangers
3. Coat hangers

_____Place hangers either in hanger hampers or freight boxes. Label boxes clearly.

_____Face hangers and hampers in the same direction to prevent tangling.

_____Organize any plexiglass by size and style.

_____Create a file for smaller signs by price point, theme, etc.

_____Check stock at cash wrap for boxes and bags.

_____Organize gift boxes on shelves by style and size, old and new. Clearly label boxes with style and size. Always use the old gift boxes first on the sales floor!

_____Organize shopping bags by style and size, old and new. Clearly label the boxes they're in by style and size. Always use the old bags first on the sales floor!

_____Organize your hardware according to their purpose (faceouts, waterfalls, etc.) and then by style and size.

_____Place fixtures in boxes, keeping all like styles together (e.g. all shelf brackets in one box, all 6" faceouts in one box, etc.) Clearly label the boxes by style and size.

_____Disassemble unused four ways, rounders, etc., and place like pieces together. Hang parts on brackets where applicable and where space permits.

_____Clean bathroom thoroughly - make it shine!

_____Clean trash can(s) thoroughly.

_____Take down any old signs, notices, etc.

_____Throw out all old supplies.

_____Clean break area - tables, chairs, etc.

_____Organize bulletin boards.

_____Clean out refrigerator and microwave if applicable.

_____Update all supplies at desk area.

_____Organize all paperwork and file it in the proper place.

_____Thoroughly clean desk, inside and out.

_____Sweep and mop the back room floor.

## CASH WRAP ORGANIZATION

_____Clean terminal thoroughly. Use a soft damp cloth. Do not use chemical cleaners.

_____Clean desk thoroughly, inside and out. Remove tape, notes, etc.

_____Organize all paper work and file it in the proper place.

_____Organize boxes by style and size.

_____Organize bags by style and size.

_____Empty hanger bins and clean thoroughly.

_____Check all holds, layaways and damages. Make sure each is clearly labeled.

_____Empty the trash. Thoroughly clean the trash can inside and out.

## SELLING FLOOR ORGANIZATION

_____Replace light bulbs if needed.

_____Clean storefront signage (CUT OFF POWER).

_____Dust hanging signs in store.

_____Clean air conditioner/heating vents. Clean ceiling tiles around vents with a duster.

_____Dust light fixtures.

_____Thoroughly clean fitting rooms. Remove all pins from carpet. Wipe/wash down doors, seating, etc. Clean mirrors.

_____Clean gate at storefront and/or sliding glass doors and tracks.

_____Wash front windows and ledges, inside and out.

_____Clean walls, one section at a time.

_____Clean any fixtures on wall section.

_____Wash/wipe baseboards.

_____Clean mirrors on selling floor.

_____Remove pins from carpet.

_____Vacuum edging around entire floor including dressing rooms and desk area.

_____Dust and clean all fixtures on the floor from top to bottom.

_____Dust accessory racks and clean thoroughly. Remove tape, marks, etc.

_____Clean all tables from top to bottom.

_____Clean any mannequins with a damp cloth. Check parts for any loose screws - tighten and repair. Report any unrepairable damage to your supervisor.

_____Dust shelves used on selling floor.

_____Thoroughly clean display cases including glass, inside, and base.

_____Clean plexi sign holders.

Sample sales contest...

## IT TAKES TEN TO WIN!

We have a new contest! It takes place over the next two weeks. Achieve the following results, and win a $50.00 gift certificate!

1. $100.00 sale

2. Item of the day - must sell one for each hour worked.

3. Units Per Transaction - 1 point for each 2 items sold. Must have minimum of 2.00 for two week period. UPT - hrs. worked = 2.00.

4. Sell Saturday feature. Sell what you're wearing.

5. $200.00 sale.

6. Most units sold in a single sale, (only one person can win this).

7. Sell the color you're wearing.

8. Must sell 1 complete outfit: top, bottom and an accessory - this means it must be for 1 person, and must match!

9. Sell a regular priced sweater.

10. Sell a pair of regular priced denim.

In case no one achieves all 10, your name will go into a hat for each time you achieve one of the above. The name drawn will win a $30.00 gift certificate!

GOOD LUCK!!!!

# LOOKING AHEAD

As the year 2000 approaches, many smaller retailers will disappear. Large chains throughout the country as well as fewer department stores will dominate the market. Stores must offer excellent customer service - both in the form of the employees they train, and advanced technology such as point of sale terminals. We must know what goods the customers want, and have the capability to support them quickly. We must have/design an effective means to reach our customer. Whether it's through home shopping channels, catalogs - print or video, newspaper, radio, television or other ad medium, our message must be clear, consise, easily recognizable, and stand out in a crowd.

Since leisure time will be decreasing, entertainment while shopping will become more important. The petting zoos of yesterday will continue to be replaced by carousels, video walls, and even amusement rides.

Store locations in power centers and regional malls will continue to prevail, as one-stop shopping becomes a viable convenience customers seek out.

# Common Sense to Retailing

## Order Form

Did you borrow this manual? Why not order your own so you can highlight or underline? Special discounts for quantity purchases.

Postal orders:

The Retail Press
P. O. Box 12554
Columbia, SC 29211

Make checks payable in U. S. funds to The Retail Press.

| **Qty.** | **Name of book** | **Price Each** | **in SC 5% tax** | **Shipping** | **Total** |
|---|---|---|---|---|---|
| ____ | **Common Sense to Retailing** | **$9.95** | ______ | **3.00** | _____ |

Please print your complete mailing address below:

Name: ________________________________________

Organization or Company: ________________________

Address: ______________________________________

City, State, Zip: _________________________________

Phone number: (_____) _____ -________________